Summer Nature Activities for Children

Items s.
Items r
or by
websi
numbe
items
loss or it

r

21.

28.

Irmgard Kutsch and Brigitte Walden

Summer Nature Activities for Children

Floris Books

Translated by Jane R. Helmchen

First published in German in 2001 as
Natur-Kinder-Garten-Werkstatt: Sommer,
by Verlag Freies Geistesleben, Stuttgart
First published in English in 2007 by
Rudolf Steiner College Press, California
and Floris Books, Edinburgh

Publication of this book has been made possible
by a grant from the Waldorf Curriculum Fund.

British Library CIP Data available

ISBN: 978-086315-586-4

Produced in Poland by Polskabook

AUGUST

Foreword

About twenty years ago, I participated in a seminar during which Dr Hans Müller-Wiedemann, an experienced doctor and teacher, made explicit the connection between a particular boy's aggressive behaviour and his lack of a basic sense of touch. It was an important moment for me. During the following weeks and months, I worked on an essay — unpublished, in the end — about the sense of touch in relation to the teachings of Rudolf Steiner. I continued to write about developmental psychology and in the early nineties began to publish the results.

Understanding the senses is essential at the therapeutic institute where I work, where we offer remedial teaching, occupational therapy and counselling, among other therapies. I have also tried to influence public debate on education, where the senses — the sense of movement and space, or the sense of balance, for example — are often overstimulated and thereby dulled.

It's in this context that we can talk about the importance of giving children a hands-on experience of nature: the elements, plants and animals. This is key to the healthy development of the senses, and is often what is missing from city and suburban lifestyles. I'm always on the look out, therefore, for people, initiatives and projects which seek to do this kind of work, and when I met Irmgard Kutsch last year, and heard about the Children's Nature and Garden Centre, I knew that I found something special.

The Centre, and this series of books, is putting into practice the ideas that I have long championed. When someone asks me, "but what can we practically do?" I don't hesitate to pull out the

Centre's address, or refer them to these books. One of the best things is that Irmgard Kutsch and Brigitte Walden's ideas and activities are universal, and can be successfully used no matter what the philosophical background or tradition of parent or teacher.

This is a quote from one of my recent books:

> I do not dream about going back
> to the "good old days." That leads
> nowhere. But for the sake of chil-
> dren, we must say: enough! Enough
> machines. Enough speed. Enough
> concrete. Enough overstimulat-
> ing flashing images. Enough things
> that feel like nothing. The everyday
> world — overwhelmed by machines
> and images, cemented together and
> covered with plastic, screaming and

addicted to speed, which can only be defended as harmless by those whose senses have already been dulled — is a disaster for the healthy development of our children, for their security and self-confidence. Ecology and education must be on the same side: to oppose environmental destruction and the suppression of nature. We cannot turn back time, but kindergartens, schools and wider society must give children back their right to experience nature first hand. To move forward in this direction requires courage, experimentation and leaving behind our familiar ruts.

Irmgard Kutsch and Brigitte Walden have shown this courage. We must follow their example.

Henning Köhler

8

The Story of This Book

Strengthening a child's will

This is Toby, and he's four years old. He is fascinated by the giant rain barrel at the Children's Nature and Garden Centre, and he loves to pump water into the watering can. With a lot of patience and skill, he has managed to clamp the watering can firmly between the pump and the edge of the barrel. This means he has both hands free: one to hold on to the barrel, and the other to move the pump handle up and down.

His strong will, and his delight in succeeding at a difficult task with objects made for adults, is plain to see. The funny noise of the pump, and the water that ultimately flows out of the watering can and back into the barrel, keep him motivated to pump again and again with great concentration and patience.

This is just one of many examples where we have seen children develop physically, mentally and emotionally through contact with natural materials and objects. It was for this reason that the Children's Nature and Garden Centre was founded, and is also the reason that we have produced this set of four books of seasonal nature activities for children — *Spring, Summer, Autumn* and *Winter*.

We hope you find our work helpful and encouraging.

Irmgard Kutsch

An Invitation

We invite you to discover a world of wonders: a living space full of stones, plants and animals of countless colours and shapes. This is a place where the sun sometimes shines, and the rain sometimes falls; where the wind blows and the clouds float by. This is a garden in which young and old can come together to build a clay oven or a willow hut, carve a walking stick, wash wool, pick fragrant herbs and nibble on delicious berries.

An inspiring environment like this makes us ask certain questions:

— How will our world look in twenty or forty years?
— What skills do our children need to learn to grow into healthy, confident adults?

— How can adults working with children learn more about nature?
— What kind of training do adults need to be able to teach children practical skills?

I have worked with children, teenagers and adults for more than thirty years, and in that time I've seen ever-increasing numbers of children with developmental, observational and movement difficulties, as well as extreme behavioural problems and language deficits. There are many causes, but a central one is our "virtual" world — of television and computer games, for example — which encourages children to experience things only through their senses of seeing and hearing, rather than through touch. Only through touch can we truly experience the world.

It's for this reason that, at the Children's Nature and Garden Centre, children climb high trees, look into deep wells and make mud pies. Adults from around the world and from all walks of life are always on hand as interested and encouraging helpers, each bringing their own cultural background, traditions and religions to the Centre. The children have amazing imaginations, flexibility, joy, courage and desire to be active. The adults help to create a space where the children can develop healthy bodies, alert minds and sensitive feelings.

By working explicitly with the different seasons, we help to ground children in the real world.

Some people think that children and tools don't mix, but at the Centre we believe that, with careful, experienced adult supervision, children can be taught to use knives and saws, pointed drills and scissors, sturdy rakes and spades, to actively develop their practical abilities. There is no pretending here: everyone is allowed to participate in

real work, and through that their sense of responsibility grows.

Singing can help maintain the rhythm of even the most strenuous work, and stories — told in a cosy place — enrich the overall experience. Holistic projects can combine central human needs such as food, clothing and housing. Activities such as planting a garden, caring for animals, working with the elements — fire, water, air and earth — and working in different outdoor settings can strengthen children physically and hone their observation skills and emotions. Handicrafts are good for training motor skills. Rhythmic language games and chants, accompanying the work, support new language skills. Above all, children develop a positive attitude to work.

The Centre has many supporters, both far and wide and close at hand, from all generations and all backgrounds. This mix of experience means that children learn to live together in acceptance and harmony. With everyone's help, educational projects that were previously stand-alone islands have been joined together in a strong network. Descartes' principle of "I think, therefore I am" has been expanded through these new links to become "I participate, therefore I am."

Ours is not a "back to nature" movement that condemns technology and progress out of hand. We all rely, to an extent, on the blessings and opportunities they can bring. Rather, our intention is to encourage awareness of the importance of our connection to nature, so that we can live in harmony with our world.

June

Working with Herbs

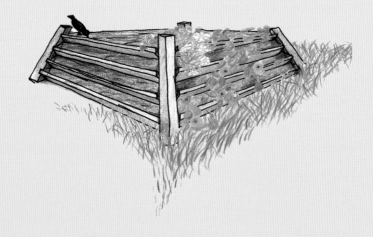

In June, in our part of the world, the sun reaches its highest point: the summer solstice. It floods nature with light, providing warmth and making everything shine. Under the zodiac sign of Gemini the twins (♊), growth is at its peak. Plant buds open and field, forest and garden are filled with an array of flowers in all colours and shapes, often accompanied by wonderful fragrances.

Back in springtime, under the signs of Aries the ram (♈), Taurus the bull (♉) and Gemini the twins (♊), plant development was outward-looking as shoots and buds grew rapidly; now, under the sign of Cancer the crab (♋), everything turns inward. The male and female elements of the plant come together and the first signs of fruit formation appear. The Cancer symbol is ideal for this time of the year, representing the turning point just past the solstice as the sun cycle changes.

In earlier times, people collected healing and flavourful herbs shortly before the solstice, because the healing properties were considered to be at their strongest. We can learn a lot from historic drawings, writings and medicinal collections. The ancient Egyptian priest-doctors knew a great deal about herbs and their properties, as did Hippocrates and Pliny, whose notes formed the basis of European medieval herbal knowledge. Monks and nuns such as Hildegard of Bingen, and doctors such as Paracelsus, maintained and developed this knowledge, planting herb gardens and learning from travellers, shepherds and herbalists.

Although they could only have guessed at how the healing properties worked, it is amazing how confidently they used the power of the herbs. It wasn't until about a century ago that Sebastian Kneipp mapped out the chemical substances in plants, and analyzed and categorized them by their healing abilities.

Used correctly, healing herbs can do no harm. They are best used to support health rather than cure illness. The well-known kitchen herbs are most appropriate for this and should be added regularly to food. Every kindergarten and school kitchen should have access to fresh herbs, preferably from the school's own garden. We recommend building a herb spiral for this purpose.

The Herb Garden

Herbs can be used in many ways. Often they are both healing and seasoning plants, whose essential oils and other components offer distinct fragrances and flavours. Fragrant herbs can have positive effects on feelings, and are useful in health care. In the garden, they are good for attracting insects and enhance the health of the soil.

– Planting a herb bed

Many kitchen herbs come from the Mediterranean, and grow best in full sun. Bearing this in mind, a south-facing bed is a good place to position a herb garden. In addition, stones used to build walls around the bed will absorb and retain extra heat.

Preparations for planting the bed should be made in the autumn when the ground is porous and rich in humus. You should not need to regularly add fertilizer to the soil, which can affect the taste of the herbs. However, you can mix heavy earth with sand to make it more porous; or mix stones into the soil for plants which flourish on dry stone walls. Some herbs love calcium, and calcium-rich stones can also be mixed in where needed. When planning your herb garden, try to position large or bushy plants at the back of the bed so they don't get in the way of the smaller plants. You should plant annual and biennial herbs in the spring.

– The herb spiral

Although some herbs like sunshine and a dry position, others need shade, damp ground, or even shallow water. A herb spiral can provide appropriate living conditions for a variety of smaller plants.

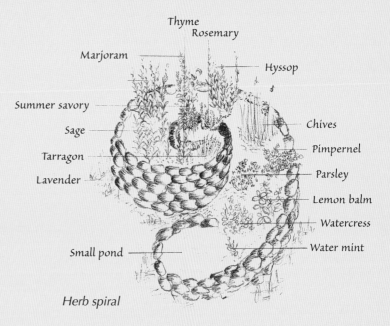

Herb spiral

First, build the surrounding dry stone wall in a sunny spot. Fill the inside with calcium-rich stones. Put a thin layer of topsoil in the upper part of the spiral, for those herbs, like thyme, which enjoy warmth. Fill the lower section with garden soil and compost; herbs which need some shade and more nourishment, such as parsley, can be planted in this area. At the foot of the spiral, make a small pond for water-loving plants such as watercress and water mint.

Lavender is a popular butterfly plant

The herb alphabet: a selection of the most important fragrant, healing and cooking herbs

	Usage	Height and growth	Propagation	Harvest	Soil and position	Special characteristics
Oregano	Fragrance (F) Healing (H) Cooking (C)	Large (L) High (H) Wide (W)	Seed (S) Division (D) Cutting (C) Root system (R)			
Annual herbs						
Basil	C	6–24 in (15–60 cm)	S from May, light	VI–VIII	humus, airy, sun, warm	insect food, hard to grow
Borage	C	up to 32 in (80 cm), L, H, W	S from April, self-seeding	V–IX	nutrient-rich, calcium, sun	bee food, edible flowers, needs space
Chamomile	F, H	8–20 in (20–50 cm)	S from April	V–X	sun	insect food
Chervil	C	12–20 in (30–50 cm)	S from March	V–X	damp (otherwise early flowers)	insect food
Dill	C	20–48 in (50–120 cm)	after April, under foil	IV–VI bef. flowering	calcium, warm	
Marigold	H	12–20 in (30–50 cm)	after March, self-seeding	VI–VIII	any position	insect and animal food
Marjoram	F, H, C	up to 20 in (50 cm)	S after May	VII–IX bef. flowering	porous soil, warm	
Nasturtium	C	up to 12 in (30 cm)	S after end April	VI–IX	any position, frost-sensitive	edible flowers
Summer savory	H, C	12–20 in (30–50 cm)	S	IV–VII	any position	
Biennial herbs						
Caraway	H, C	12–24 in (30–60 cm)	S after April, light	VI–IX	deep in ground, damp	not good with fennel
Parsley	C	up to 12 in (30 cm)	S after March	IV–XII	humus, damp, partial shade	
Winter cress or yellow rocket	C	12–24 in (30–60 cm)	S spring and late summer	V–XII	damp, loam	harvest in winter too
Perennial herbs						
Chives	C	8–12 in (20–30 cm)	S after March, D	IV–X	calcium, damp, partial shade	lovely flavour, replant frequently

	Usage	Height and growth	Propagation Seed (S)	Harvest	Soil and position	Special characteristics
	Fragrance (F) Healing (H) Cooking (C)	Large (L) High (H) Wide (W)	Division (D) Cutting (C) Root system (R)			

Perennial herbs (cont.)

	Usage	Height and growth	Propagation	Harvest	Soil and position	Special characteristics
Comfrey	H	20–40 in (50–100 cm), L	S in spring, D	IV–VI	any position	insect food, deep roots, fertilizer
Fennel	H, C	32–80 in (80–200 cm), H	S	VIII–IX	calcium, sun, nutrient-rich	insect food
Horse-radish	H, C	up to 48 in (120 cm), spreads	S in March, plant root year before	XII–III, root	humus, damp, deep in ground	good for yeast infections
Hyssop	F, H, C (esp. gravy)	16–24 in (40–60 cm)	D, C	VII–X	loose, dry	insect food
Lavender	F, H, C	12–24 in (30–60 cm), W	S, C	VI–VII, for healing bef. flowering	calcium, dry, sun	insect food, lovely fragrance
Lovage	C	up to 70 in (180 cm), L, H, W	S, D	V–X	damp, partial shade	
Mint	F, H, C	16–32 in (40–80 cm), L, W, spreads	R, cut back every 2–3 years	VI–X	humus, damp	insect food, spreads
Mugwort	H, C	20–40 in (50–100 cm), L	S in spring, D	VI–X	any position	
Oregano	C	8–20 in (20–50 cm), W	D, R	VII–X	warm, dry, calcium	insect food, cut back aft. flowering
Pimpernel	F, H, C	12–24 in (30–60 cm)	D	V–X	any position	replant every few years
Rosemary	C	20–60 in (50–150 cm), H, W	C	IV–VI	humus, sun, porous, calcium	protect during winter
Sage	F, H, C	16–28 in (40–70 cm), W	D, C	VI–X	humus, sun, porous	insect food, protect during winter
Sorrel	F, H, C	12–32 in (30–80 cm)	S, D		always damp	
Southern-wood or Boy's love	C	32–40 in (80–100 cm), L	D, C		calcium, humus, dry	good border plant, fragrance repels insects
Tarragon	F, H, C	24–60 in (60–150 cm)	R	V–IX	damp, warm	fertilizer, protect during winter
Thyme	F, H, C	up to 12 in (30 cm)	S, D, C	V–VII	dry, sun, calcium, rock garden	
Winter savory	F, H, C	12–20 in (30–50 cm)	S, light, D	V–VII	any position, also rock garden	insect food

In a raised bed, tasty herbs can be easily cut fresh every day and used to make herb butter, herb cheese, herb oil, herb salt and many other delicious things

We have a sweet cicely (*myrrhis odorata*) plant growing in the corner of our garden. My children call it the "licorice plant" and every now and then they love to pick a leaf and smell the strong aniseed fragrance. Child-like investigation and discovery is the natural basis for working with herbs: whether it be lemon balm, oregano or mint, the strong smells given off by many herbs naturally arouse children's curiosity and delight.

Working with herbs is also a great way to teach children about the origin of food and how food is made, rather than seeing food as something that comes out of the freezer or from fast-food restaurants. If children are given an opportunity to plant and harvest herbs for themselves, and then play their part in turning them into a meal, they are learning important values of independence and responsibility that will greatly help the future of our world.

Dr Gero Karthaus, ecologist and author

20

Raised Beds for Herbs

Our experience shows that children and their parents really enjoy working with herbs, and often go on to plant herb beds at home where possible. If space is limited at home, pots, troughs and raised beds can be useful; see, for example the description of the "Paradise" balcony garden in the April chapter of the *Spring* book in this series.

Working with Herbs: Basic Skills

Herbs in their natural surroundings can provide so many rich experiences for children that other more artificial teaching approaches are rendered redundant. Spend time exploring the most basic characteristics of the plants: the different leaf shapes, the different colours and the different smells.

If there's enough space, hilly beds with lots of sunlight are very good for herbs

Using sloping posts at the corners can mean more light and water for the plants growing out the side; however a bed like this is more difficult to build

Children who are used to growing and handling herbs will soon, with adult help, be able to use them safely and independently in cooking. Ideally, kindergartens and schools should involve children in making fresh daily snacks with herbs that the whole class can enjoy eating together (see also the August chapter in this book, and the September chapter in the *Autumn* book).

Working with herbs involves all the senses: through looking, smelling, tasting and touching, children learn about the plants in an entirely natural way

Raised beds are ideal for children and are easy to build. You can get up to fifty square feet (five square metres) of planting space on just three square feet (one square metre) of ground. Build the side boards at an angle to allow for side planting; these plants are easy to see and care for.

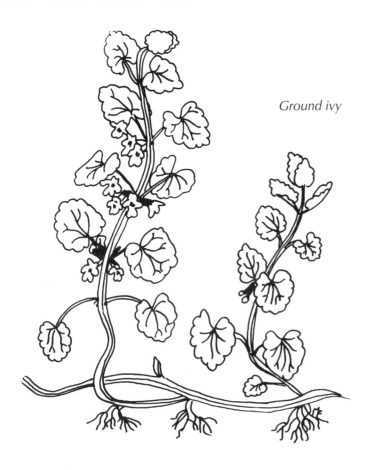

Ground ivy

Herb Recipes

Children can help to make all these recipes. Feel free to vary the recipes and experiment!

⌐ Garden herb butter

Finely chop a handful of freshly picked and washed garden herbs such as tarragon, thyme, marjoram, rosemary, lovage, chives, garlic, spring onion, parsley, chervil, hyssop or winter savory. Add them to half a pound of butter and mix thoroughly. Add salt to taste.

⌐ Ground ivy butter

Beat some butter until creamy, then add salt to taste and finely chopped ground ivy leaves. Leave to stand before serving with fresh bread; it looks lovely decorated with a small ground ivy sprig.

⌐ Garden herb cottage cheese or quark

This is excellent served with fresh bread or potatoes. Mix 2 tablespoons of cream, a teaspoon of salt, the juice of half a lemon and one finely chopped onion with 1 lb (500 g) of cottage cheese or quark, and enough milk to make the mixture spreadable. Mix in a selection of garden herbs as in the "Garden herb butter" recipe.

⁓ Wild herb cottage cheese or quark

Many wild herbs can be found on a countryside walk. Season the cheese with lots of garlic and some sorrel, willowherb and ribwort; you can also add a bit of lovage from the garden, and salt to taste.

⁓ Herb oil

This is very good served on leafy salads. In a bottle, mix up good quality sunflower, olive or thistle oil with very dry twigs of tarragon, hyssop, marjoram, thyme, lovage or winter savory, and perhaps some

Children love nutritious bread and butter decorated with freshly cut herbs or sprinkled with herb salt. Peppermint tea goes especially well with this easy and cheap snack.

Sewing a little bag and filling it with lavender helps develop motor skills, concentration and problem-solving

garlic. Ensure the twigs are well covered by the oil, otherwise they'll go mouldy. Leave the herb oil for several weeks then strain it, using a funnel, into a clean bottle, leaving the herb sticks behind.

⇥ Herb salt

Use a pestle and mortar for this recipe. Put one tablespoon of good quality sea salt in the mortar and add a small amount of assorted dried herbs left over from last year. Grind them into the salt. Combine this mixture with another 1/2 lb (250 g) of salt and seal the container well. Delicious with home-made bread (see the August chapter).

⇥ Herb pancakes

Makes twelve pancakes. Mix 1 1/2 lb (750 g) of flour, six eggs, 1 quart (1 l) of milk and three teaspoons of salt with one cup (two good handfuls) of freshly chopped herbs. Leave to stand for half an hour. Spoon into a hot greased frying pan to cook — if possible, over an open fire.

⇥ Cream cheese with wild herbs

Season the cream cheese with salt and pepper to taste and add finely chopped mustard leaves, nettle flowers and nettle seeds. Decorate with clover and willowherb.

⇥ Spelt and wild herb spread

Spelt is a type of wheat crop found in Central Europe. In Germany, the unripe grains are often dried and eaten as a healthy alternative to wheat. This recipe uses ground spelt, which is also an excellent bread-making flour.

Cook 3 1/2 oz (100 g) of medium ground spelt in 1 quart (1 l) of vegetable stock until soft. Add salt and pepper to taste, and a roughly chopped onion, while the mixture is still warm. Finally, mix in finely chopped goutweed or bishop's weed to taste.

⇥ Rhubarb and ground ivy jam

Cook 1 lb (500 g) of rhubarb in a little water. Add 1/2 lb (250 g) of sugar and a handful of ground ivy leaves. Bring to the boil briefly then pour into jars to set.

⇥ Strawberries with sage

This has an unusual but sensational taste. Pick fresh strawberries and sage leaves from the garden; you'll need about twenty sage leaves for every pound (500 g) of strawberries. Mix and sweeten with honey to taste.

Elder

⌐ *Elderflower juice*

Mix 10 quarts (10 l) of water with ten elderflower heads, three sliced, unwaxed lemons, and 1/2 pint (250 ml) of vinegar. Leave to infuse for two days, stirring from time to time. Sweeten to taste with honey or sugar and serve chilled.

⌐ *Elderflower and raspberry vinegar*

The first raspberries are usually ripening at the same time as the last elderflowers appear. This is the time to put a large cup (three generous handfuls) of raspberries and an elderflower head into a bottle. Fill up the bottle with a fruit vinegar. After four to six weeks, try a small sample: in a glass, mix a dash of the vinegar with honey and fill up with cold water. This is a wonderful thirst-quencher!

⌐ *Rosebud vinegar*

Use the same recipe as above, substituting rosebuds for the elderflower and raspberries. Also delicious.

⌐ *Rose sugar*

Dry two handfuls of fragrant rose petals, then crumble them into a fine powder and mix with about 1/2 lb (250 g) of sugar. It will smell wonderful. Rose sugar can be used in many drinks and recipes such as tea, sweet sauces, cakes and yoghurt.

⌐ *Wild herb salad*

Many herbs can be found on a countryside walk that will make a delicious salad. Look especially for daisies, garlic, nettles, chickweed, sorrel, willowherb, ground ivy, comfrey, goutweed, dandelion and ribwort. Don't eat any plant you're unsure about and only pick the best leaves, so you don't

Peppermint stalks are bound together in thin bundles and hung on a frame until completely dry

have to sort them later. Wash them quickly, place in a large bowl and decorate with dandelions, daisies and clover. Dress with oil, vinegar, honey, salt and pepper and serve immediately.

Sage or nettle "mice"

Mix two eggs with 1/2 lb (250 g) of flour, a pinch of salt and some milk to make a batter. Dip fresh sage or nettle leaves, with their stems left on, into the batter and fry in a greased pan. The batter bubbles up during cooking which makes them look like little mice, with the stems as the tails. Sprinkle with sugar and cinnamon before serving hot.

Wild herb stew

Pick two handfuls of fresh young wild herbs such as ribwort, sorrel, yarrow, goutweed and nettle, and wash and chop them. Gently fry two small chopped onions in butter and add 2 lb (1 kg) of peeled, diced potatoes. Cover with hot vegetable stock so the potatoes are completely submerged

and simmer gently, allowing the liquid to reduce. When the potatoes are nearly cooked, add the herbs to the mixture along with milk or cream and salt and pepper to taste.

This recipe is also good when made using only chives, or only nettles.

Cough tea

Cut two clean ribwort leaves into small pieces and cover with boiling water. Allow to infuse for ten minutes then sweeten with honey to taste. Drink three glasses a day to help treat a cough.

Ribwort cough syrup

Boil 1 lb (500 g) of brown sugar in 1 pint (500 ml) of water and add two generous handfuls of ribwort leaves torn into small pieces. Simmer for twenty minutes then pour into jars while still hot and allow to cool. Take two teaspoons, three times a day, to help treat a cough.

Boiled onion cough syrup

Simmer 1 lb (500 g) of onions with 1 lb (500 g) of brown sugar in 1 1/4 pint (600 ml) of water. In days gone by, this cough medicine used to stand permanently on the back of the stove where it was kept just warm. One teaspoon taken two to three times a day in warm milk can work wonders.

Raw onion cough syrup

Put some fresh onion rings in a jar and sprinkle sugar over them. Leave them to stand in a warm place until liquid appears. Take one to two teaspoons of the liquid three times a day. It helps to relieve the impulse to cough, and allows the patient to sleep.

➤ Marigold ointment

Melt 1/2 lb (250 g) of pork lard and add two handfuls of marigold (calendula) flowers. Allow the fat to cover the flower heads. Leave to stand overnight then heat gently and strain. Pour the liquid into jars and cool. This is a good ointment for irritated skin and small cuts.

➤ Sage cough drops

Gently heat 1/2 lb (250 g) of sugar in a small pan until melted, then add twenty finely chopped sage leaves. Stir well. Use two spoons to form individual drops of the sticky mixture, and place on greased waxed paper to cool. The sugar helps these drops to taste good, although it's actually better just to suck on a fresh sage leaf.

➤ Tea

There are lots of herbal teas of course, but we especially recommend peppermint or lemon balm tea. Right before making the tea, get the children to cut two or three fresh stalks of the herb from the garden. Place the stalks in a 2 quart (2 l) teapot and cover with boiling water. This tea will taste far more aromatic than anything bought from the supermarket.

Sage should not be missing from the tea herb bed. Cut off the fresh shoots before the buds develop (which can be as early as mid-May) and bind them together into thin bundles, or place them on cloths, to dry. You can make the tea in advance and pour it into dark jars to be saved for cold winter days when the children are coughing and sneezing. Only use a small amount of sage, otherwise the tea will be too strong. Only when the tea has cooled to drinking temperature should you sweeten with honey; this helps preserve the healing properties of the sage.

Marigold, Calendula officinalis, *and peppermint (below right)*

June

Breeding Butterflies

Butterflies: a Symbol of Beauty

It's often children who notice the first butterfly of spring. In our part of the world it's usually a bright yellow Brimstone, called to life in early March by the warming sun. Along with snowdrops and crocuses, it's a sure sign of the new season approaching.

Butterflies are symbols of beauty, complexity and fragility. Their metamorphosis from caterpillar, through the crysalis stage, to adult insect is a wonderful opportunity for us to learn about a complex natural process, and to consider the meaning of beauty and ugliness.

Above all, the butterfly is a compelling illustration of the unbreakable link between a living creature and its habitat. Children quickly understand that the colourful meadows and hedgerows are major fuelling stations for butterflies, and that protecting these spaces is vitally important. These are wonderful lessons to learn in kindergarten.

Dr Gero Karthaus

Looking after Caterpillars

Butterflies are amongst the most colourful creatures in nature. Children and adults alike love finding these fluttering works of art in the garden or meadow. A steady destruction of their natural habitats, and the use of pollutants like insecticides, however, means that many species are disappearing. It's estimated that up to one third of European butterflies are facing extinction. Breeding butterflies and releasing them into the wild has never been more important.

The task is a large one. The Peacock and Small Tortoiseshell butterflies, for example, lay around 150 eggs but only one or two butterflies, able to reproduce, will successfully survive into adulthood. We must protect butterflies from their natural predators as well as from bad weather. Caterpillars, chrysalizes and butterflies serve as food for many kinds of birds, and caterpillars often fall foul of other parasitic insects. Caterpillars are

31

also very sensitive to damp, cold and wind; we can care for them by providing a dry, light and airy environment, and food.

A Butterfly's Favourite Places

We have to make sure that, when we release the butterflies into the wild, there are enough of the right type of food plants in the immediate area to sustain them. The plants could be in our own garden, our neighbour's garden, or in open fields. Particularly good plants for butterflies include: snowdrops, spring snowflakes, hyacinths, crocuses, aubrieta, knapweed, phacelia, hutchinsia, marigolds (calendula), yarrow, chamomile, cosmea, echinacea, scabious, wallflowers, sedum, carnations, fuchsia, alyssum and asters.

Some of our fragrant herbs, when allowed to flower, serve as excellent butterfly nourishment. These include lavender, borage, caraway, thyme, chervil, hyssop, lovage, sage, marjoram, dill and winter savory.

Simple grasslands with a variety of wild flower species are also ideal. Plants here would include chicory, oregano, wild carrot, St John's wort,

5

7

1 Small Tortoiseshell

2 Peacock

3 Red Admiral

4 Map (outer wing)

5 Map (inner wing)

6 Heavily magnified view of Peacock butterfly eggs on a nettle leaf

7 The eggs are packed tightly together. This photograph shows empty egg casings on a dried nettle leaf, magnified to ×10

A particularly popular butterfly plant is the buddleia, or butterfly bush, to which many different butterflies will be attracted. Having this plant in your garden gives children the best possible chance of seeing wild butterflies close up.

Nettles are the most important food plant for a whole group of caterpillar species. Allow them to grow in a seldom-used part of the garden.

It might be difficult for some kindergartens or schools to provide such a range of flowers throughout the year. If so, reach out into your community for volunteers of all ages to help maintain a garden, or get in touch with a local ecology group who might be able to help. Children get so few opportunities to see the whole life cycle of a butterfly that it's really worth trying every option.

vetches, daisies, clovers, bedstraw and knapweed.

Many hedge plants are excellent sources of butterfly food. These include daphne, black elderberry, wild rose, sloe, hawthorn, buckthorn, broom, raspberries, blackberries, hazlenut, willow, cherry laurel and honeysuckle.

From Caterpillar to Butterfly

The first butterfly eggs are normally found around the start of May. With young children, it can be best to breed simple caterpillars such as the Small Tortoiseshell (1) or Peacock (2). If you can find them, the Red Admiral (3) and Map (4 and 5) butterflies can also work well.

6

The "guest room" for the Peacock eggs was placed between the inner and outer windows, in a space about 10 inches (25 cm) wide

Small Tortoiseshell caterpillars with yellow and green stripes

Peacock caterpillars, black with silver dots

Butterfly eggs are most commonly found on the underside of nettle leaves, since this is where the caterpillar will feed. The female butterfly will lay 100–250 eggs in a single mass. Look out for a leaf with yellowish brown holes in the midst of otherwise perfectly healthy green leaves.

In some cases, tiny caterpillars will already have emerged from the eggs and will have started to feed. This makes them even easier to find; look for the devastated plants (the photographs on the left show nettle plants where caterpillars have munched right down to the stalks). When the caterpillars get bigger, we can start to distinguish

The Peacock caterpillars can be seen here in various phases: caterpillars looking for a good place to go into the cocoon stage; caterpillars hanging, heads down, shortly before becoming a cocoon; fresh cocoons in green; and older grey cocoons.

Peacock butterflies slipping out of their cocoon

their patterns. The Small Tortoiseshell caterpillar has yellow and black lengthways stripes, while the Peacock caterpillar is black with tiny silver dots.

One summer at the Children's Nature and Garden Centre, we successfully bred about 150 butterflies. We discovered the eggs during a walk, clustered on a nettle plant, and carefully carried them in a cloth back to the Centre. We put the eggs in a vase with more nettles in a warm place on the window sill, between our inner and outer windows. The area was lined with paper towels, which were changed daily to avoid infection from dirt and excrement. A screen with tiny holes was set up to protect the creatures when the window was open.

A few dry nettle branches, placed in water, were enough for the first few days. As soon as the caterpillars hatched and began to feed, however, larger bundles of juicy nettles were needed. The caterpillars spun a fine, sticky thread in a horizontal figure of eight, all over the window pane, swinging their heads back and forth rhymically while spinning. The structure was almost three feet (one metre) high, and the thread also joined up the nettle leaves, like a kind of ladder. When a new branch was introduced, the caterpillars quickly moved onto it. Some of them had to be helped over using a thin paintbrush; for others, we cut off the old leaf the caterpillar was attached to, and put it on the new branch. Every day, they ate more and more.

The tiny caterpillars found on May 21 had turned into cocoons by June 15. First they found

a spot out of direct sunlight, and attached the back end of their bodies to the ceiling with a thickly spun thread (in the wild, they attach to the underside of branches). They hung, head down, almost motionless, for a day or two. Then the drama began. They writhed until the prickly black caterpillar fur cracked, and a fresh green creature became visible underneath. The old skin was stripped off, along with the eyes and legs, and the delicate cocoon appeared.

On June 30, the miracle happened. A cocoon broke open, and a shrivelled, wrinkled and bud-like creature appeared, crawling upwards to get more air under its wings. Blood was pumped into the wings, and as they grew stronger, they became more colourful.

We removed the fine mesh screen so that the butterflies could go free. After a couple of hours — or in some cases, the next day — the butterfly would tremble, then attempt its first flight. Sometimes we helped it with a paintbrush to get more air under its wings.

It's hard to describe how the beautiful sight of 150 Peacock butterflies, launching themselves into nature, affected the children. They watched in total amazement. So did the adults.

Butterflies live amongst the flowers for about six weeks. After that, the whole cycle of repro-duction starts again.

Making a Butterfly Cage

Not everyone has a handy inner window sill they can use to breed butterflies. However, you can makie a butterfly cage from a crate or an old nightstand (bedside table). Don't be tempted to use a fish aquarium, because there's no air cir-culation.

This cage is best made from very thin plywood. You need to make sure it shuts well, so that the caterpillars can't escape through the gaps. The sides of the cage are made from a fine mesh with holes no larger than 1/50 inch (0.5 mm).

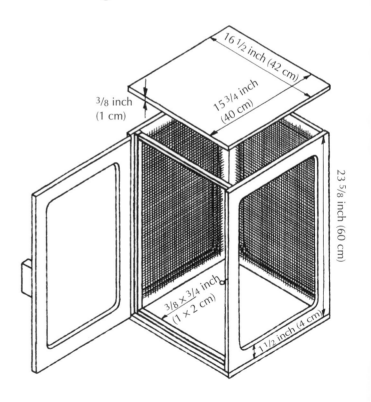

The first butterfly of spring is often the yellow Brimstone. Here, it is dipping its proboscis into a flower.

Butterflies

Butterflies go fluttering by
On coloured wings that catch the eye
On wings of orange and silvery blue
On wings of golden yellow, too.
Butterflies float in the air
Making their homes almost anywhere:
The rainforest, field and prairie land,
On mountaintops and desert sand.

Emerging on the winds of spring
Beautiful butterflies on the wing.

Shy Little Caterpillar

A shy little caterpillar looked at the sky.
He hugged a leaf stem and he gave a big sigh.
The sky and the stem didn't give a reply;
He didn't understand and he didn't know why.

He hid from the birds so quick and so sly.
He hid from the ant family living close by.
"Please, little caterpillar, why are you shy?
Please, little caterpillar, try not to cry."

"I'll try," said the caterpillar, "but I *am* shy.
I wouldn't be shy if I could just fly.
I know what I'm going to do, by and by:
I'll spin a fine bed and then say goodbye."

A little wind sang him a sweet lullaby.
And when he woke up, his wet wings were dry.
The shy little caterpillar whispered, "Goodbye."
He flew to the sky and was no longer shy
Because he'd become a beautiful butterfly!

The Swallowtail butterfly has become increasingly rare. It's remarkable for its colouring and size. ➤

July

Earth, Water, Air and Fire

At the height of summer, all our senses can appreciate the fullness and beauty of nature

By July, summer is in full swing. Splendid flower displays draw us out into fields, woods and gardens, their fine fragrances filling the warm air. Scents like those from flowers work directly on our bodies, entering our metabolism with each breath. Childhood smells are something that stay with us for the rest of our lives, conjuring up memories even in old age.

Our sense of smell is less sensitive than it used to be because of frequent overstimulation. Even a good sales clerk in a perfume shop will advise that "less is more." So avoid the new children's perfumes starting to appear on the market and take children outside, instead, to experience some of nature's most wonderful scents.

Plant growth under the zodiac sign of Gemini the twins (♊) now leads to fruit and seed formation under the sign of Cancer the crab (♋). Attentive observers will notice new buds forming for the coming growth cycle.

Around this time, young birds leave their nests and become more and more independent in looking for food. Young hedgehogs wander through the garden in the evening. The tadpoles (pollywogs) in the pond have grown into small frogs.

People are often able to take a break from work at this time of year, and spend a lot of time outdoors. We enjoy the warmth of the sun and the fresh air, whether we're in the mountains or at the seaside.

This is a good time of year to engage with the natural elements. The ancient Greeks gave us the idea of the four classical elements: earth, water, fire and air. Many natural phenomena, such as the growth of plants, can be explored and explained through the interaction of these elements. During a storm, for example, all the elements are at work: water-bearing clouds are warmed by the sun and the wind (air) causes different temperature layers to rub against each other. The build up of friction is finally released in the form of lightning (fire) over the earth.

Our ancestors knew that life on our planet would not be possible without the combination of earth, water, fire and air. They revered the elements

"Why doesn't the wood sink?"

Water collects in a little girl's mudhole

as life-giving gods. Today, we need to show respect and responsibility for the elements, and find ways to understand and protect them.

Children cannot learn skills for handling the elements early enough. They should be taught ways of interacting with them affectionately, carefully and imaginatively; and for this, they must experience them first hand.

Water

Water holds a particular attraction for young children. They seem to be magically pulled towards puddles and streams, and they can play for hours with great patience and imagination by a river or at the seaside, diverting water or damming it up to create their own lake.

The River
Molly de Havas

I spring within a moss-grown dell
on rugged mountain land,
Where only stunted pine trees,
shallow-rooted, sparely stand,
And slow I grow with melted snow
from peaks on either hand.

I choose myself the quickest path
to find my way downhill,
And all the time from every side
new trickles swell my rill,
From sodden peat and cloudy mist
I draw their water chill.

I ripple over pebbles,
over waterfalls I leap,
I speed through narrow clefts where I
must dig my channel deep,
Then through the valley meadowlands
in placid curves I sweep.

Small fishes live within me,
in my reeds the wildfowl nest;
Kingfisher, rat and otter
in my banks may safely rest,
And all poor weary creatures
are by crystal water blest.

Sometimes my sparkling clarity
is hidden by a frown,
Of dirt and oil and rubbish
as I pass a busy town;
And sometimes little boats I bear
with sails of white or brown.

At last I reach a sandy shore
whereon great waves foam,
By nature bound, yet ever free,
I need no longer roam,
The path designed I followed
to the sea which is my home.

Water can be used very effectively in artistic projects, as described here:

A Bridge to Lie on

One day after a long hike through the mountains, I was so tired that I lay down on a bridge. I sensed the tremendous power of the water flowing beneath me, along with its purifying and calming nature. In an era when there are few opportunities to withdraw, to find a quiet place to relax and observe, this bridge seemed to me to be a natural source of strength. So I built my own bridges, over two particular brooks, and invited people to come and experience them.

Many people who lay down on one of the two bridges didn't want to get back up. Even children became very still, and enjoyed the experience. Everyone felt stimulated, calmed, relaxed or enriched in their own way.

The bridge connects with all the senses. You can hear flowing water, rustling trees, the cracking of the forest floor, and singing birds. You can feel the breeze, the coolness of the water below, the dampness, and the sunshine on your skin. You can

Many people find it calming and healing to be close to water in any of its forms

see the sky through the trees, the bush above the bridge, the insects and other small animals. You can smell the wood and grass of the bridge, the fragrance of the nearby meadow, and the fresh air.

The bridge is made from wood and rope, and covered with hay or grasses. All the materials will decompose in their own time, becoming part of nature's cycles.

Water has become an integral part of my artistic work. Another project, for example, uses falling drops of water to create musical sounds, which are associated with rain, tears, rhythm and time. Vessels filled with water radiate a calming transcendence.

Water is one of the most important elements for life and, in this time of exploitation, must be appreciated and protected.

Ute Poeppel, artist

Ute Poeppel lying on her bridge over a bubbling brook

Ponds and Streams

Many children no longer have the chance to play regularly in a babbling brook or shallow pond. It's a good idea, therefore, for kindergartens to create a small pond for children to play in. Note that this should be quite separate from a marsh or wetland habitat designed for plants and animals — also a great project.

The playing pond should have a gently slanting bank and the surface should be free from sharp stones and other hazards. Dig a shallow hole, not more than one foot (30 cm) deep. Place a layer of sand 4–5 inches (10–12 cm) thick in the hole and cover with the strongest garden pond plastic sheeting you can get. Cover the plastic with small and medium-sized smooth gravel and pebbles, so that there is only room for 4–6 inches (10–15 cm) of water. That way, the water will always be lower than the top of the smallest wellington boots (galoshes).

In accordance with official guidelines, the playing pond at the Children's Nature and Garden Centre could be up to 12 inches (30 cm) deep, but we don't recommend this because it's too dangerous for the youngest children. One and two year olds are most at risk around ponds, and can drown in even the shallowest water. We therefore recommend that anyone caring for children under the age of three should ensure that low, stable fences are securely placed around all ponds and wetlands, and that young children are never left unsupervised near water. Despite the possible dangers, the joy that children get from playing in water means that projects such as a play pond are very worthwhile.

1 Swinging over a creek on a long rope

2 A kindergarten class on a forest trip

3 A wetland habitat; the bank here would be too steep for a play pond

4 A piece of left-over plastic sheeting is quickly integrated into a new game. When the children leave, birds may also come to take a cool bath.

5 and 6 This kindergarten has built a small stream without using plastic or concrete. A hand-operated pump draws up groundwater and a meandering channel directs the water into a small pond. Over time, the water course changes and everyone joins in to rebuild and redesign.

▲▼ This play waterfall, modelled on John Wilkes' pioneering flowform design, was built in a school garden. On hot days, the younger children love playing in the bubbling water; and teachers report that they return to their classrooms regenerated and refreshed.

In the afternoon and evening during the summer, older students sit around the waterfall. It's a relaxing place to be: the temperature is comfortable, the air is pleasantly damp and there's no dust swirling around.

The whole structure uses relatively little water because it's a closed system with a pump and two small ponds. The water stays very clean because it's constantly enriched with oxygen.

Here is a very practical solution: the flowing water drains beneath a path, but is nonetheless visible. The path can still be crossed easily by toys, garden equipment and wheelchairs.

We built this brook at the Children's Nature and Garden Centre at table height for people in wheelchairs. We covered three long, narrow tables with plastic sheeting and built banks from clay, earth, stones and round pieces of wood under the sheeting, to keep the water in. We installed a small hand pump at the top end, and a basin at the lower end which is attached to the pump with a long hose. No electricity is needed so the whole structure is very mobile; it can also be raised and lowered by placing extra supports under the table legs.

This table-height stream was built in a school under the direction of Herbert Dreiseitl, an acclaimed water sculptor. It took thirty students, working as a team, less than twenty minutes to construct. And at no point did the water go over the edge!

Children can experience water in simple ways too — an old metal bowl is often enough!

▲ *A miniature living space for water plants*

◄ *First the clean water is used for playing; then it is used to wash sheep's wool (see the* Winter *book in this series). Finally it is poured onto flower beds as fertilizer.*

Water: Lessons for Life

When children learn about the value of water for life, it's not through an analysis of its chemical properties or ecological relationships. It's through practical, hands-on activity and through experiencing it with all their senses. Adults should bear this in mind when acting as role models for children: getting wet sets a much better example than just talking about water.

Where possible, kindergartens and schools should consider storing rainwater for use in the building or garden. A plant-based sewage system can prepare water for general use; and a composting toilet can transform waste into valuable fertilizer for the garden, rather than flushing it into precious drinking water. Transparent water pipes and equipment such as guttering, drainage pipes and cisterns can be great teaching tools: children can clearly see the water moving around and it gives them an insight into how much water we use on a daily basis.

Good habits learnt at kindergarten can spill over into the home: for example, if children are used to playing in a garden pond at school, they're more likely to want at least a small water tub at home (see picture opposite). In a kindergarten, it can be helpful if one teacher takes on responsibility for advising parents on such issues.

▲ *Children love participating in "real work" which involves earth, sand and stones*

Clay is especially precious if children understand where it comes from ▼

Earth

The "earth" element includes all rocks, minerals and soil. Younger children often associate with the idea of "Mother Earth" who cares for all living things. This image can therefore help children make the link between, for example, garden earth and a practical activity like growing plants.

Earth today is frequently exploited and loaded with various pollutants, or covered with concrete. It is in particular need of our attention and care.

▼ ▲ *The artistic results of one school's earth project week*

These unique creatures have been made from a clay and straw mixture

"Should I laugh or cry?" An early clay experience.

An earth corner is a useful addition to any classroom. Use it to collect together many different types of natural building materials: from fired or unfired clay slabs and cinder blocks with holes, to paving stones, gravel, plaster and broken rocks. Pretty coloured or nicely-shaped stones and pebbles, which the children find on outdoor trips, can be placed here too for use in various games.

Clay is a particularly versatile earth material. You can often find it on the banks of a river where it has been exposed by the water; after it has been dug up, you can put it through a sieve, enrich it, thin it out with sand, knead or beat it. It's good for making rough containers and various insect nesting aids, flowerpots and birdbaths (see the *Spring* book in this series for more details). Note that this type of clay is normally too coarse for use in fine ceramic projects (see the February chaper in the *Winter* book for ideas on working with clay).

Earth and gravity are closely related. A one-year-old child starting to walk must learn to overcome, and work with, the characteristics of both gravity and the earth in order to successfully walk upright. As the child gets older, games which involve jumping, hopping and skipping — in other words, liberating oneself from earth and gravity — help to develop physical strength and coordination. An extreme version of this is walking on stilts!

Finally, ball games are also very symbolic in relation to earth: balls are spheres, just like our planet. Playing with balls is beneficial activity in that it grounds children, develops their sense of space, and encourages their growing motor skills.

51

A stone labyrinth is a marvellous way for children to develop orientation skills. It also encourages them to slow down, a useful counter to their natural inclination to run.

Air

There are lots of well-known games that allow children to experience the qualities of air and wind: sailing boats on a pond, flying kites, dropping mini parachutes, blowing windmills, throwing and catching rings and balls, or watching flags flutter. The possibilities are endless. One particularly good way to experience air is through shining soap bubbles.

Older kindergarten children love playing with bows and arrows, and seeing the arrows fly smoothly through the air. Close supervision is needed for this activity! Children can also experience the air with all their senses through simple activities such as running, riding a scooter or bicycle, jumping, balancing and swinging.

We need to work hard to regain and maintain the health and purity of our water, earth and air for our generation and those to come. Otherwise, our children's children will not have the opportunity to climb a healthy tree with stable branches and life-giving leaves.

– Giant soap bubbles

Boil together 1 quart (1 l) of water, 1 1/2 oz (50 g) of sugar and 2 oz (80 g) of mild (pH-neutral) soap and leave to stand overnight. Dissolve 1 teaspoon of wallpaper glue in water and stir it into the mixture.

Make a wire ring about 6–8 inches (15–20 cm) in diameter, with a handle, and wind some woollen yarn around it. With some care, giant bubbles can be blown through the ring.

You will be able to blow bigger bubbles in humid air.

Oats and Beans

1 Oats and beans and bar - ley grow, Oats and beans and bar - ley grow, Do
2 First the far - mer sows his seed, Then he stands and takes his ease,

you or I or an - y - one know, How oats and beans and bar - ley grow?
Stamps his feet and claps his hands And turns a - round to view the land.

A merry-go-round at a summer festival — ready, get set, go! Hold on tight!

A vertical mast has been solidly anchored in the ground. At seat height, there's a revolving cross of beams; on the end of these, seats have been woven out of rope. There are extra ropes to hold on to, which are attached to the top of the mast. These ropes wind round the central mast when the cross beams are pushed round; then unravel in the opposite direction to send the merry-go-round spinning back again. There should be a safety fence all the way around.

Even five year olds (as well as fifteen and fifty year olds) love to conquer gravity by climbing as high as they can. Once up on a branch, they are often alone and can observe the world quietly from a different viewpoint — that of the birds.

Conscious Listening

There is a huge variety of noises, sounds and tones in nature. If we listen carefully, we can learn all kinds of things about the sound-maker. A bird twittering, the roar of a waterfall or the sound of the wind blowing all speak to us in a profound way. And we are supposed to listen: why else would the ear be the most sensitive organ in the human body? The world of sound is designed to enrich us mentally and emotionally, to bring us pleasure and warn us of danger.

Our modern world, however, makes it difficult for us to listen. Everything is loud and fast; everything tries to be even louder and faster. We are losing the fine tuning of our hearing, and understandably so: it's a defence mechanism against the unrelenting noise of the television or the traffic. What can be done?

I believe in encouraging a program of conscious listening, to re-learn what sound has to tell us. Conscious hearing must be trained through regular practice and experimentation. For ten years, I have been creating my own musical instruments and running music seminars, often in schools. I've

Chladni plates are covered by fine sand and a violin bow is drawn across them. The sand realigns into fine patterns depending on the tone, making the vibrations visible. See Further Reading for more information on cymatics and chladni plates.

Jochen Fassbender's "resonance swing," through which tonal vibrations can be experienced by the whole body

found that surprising sounds create curiosity in the listener, and long tones help us to listen more consciously. It can also be helpful to experience sound with other senses: chladni plates — whereby a bow is run across a surface with sand on it to produce different patterns depending on the tone — make sound vibrations stunningly visible (see above). Equally, it's good to be able to *feel* a vibrating resonance through our sense of touch (sometimes by lying down on one — see left).

55

This brings us to an important aspect of resonance. A sounding rod held over an empty vessel with air at the same frequency will result in a strong resonance. This phenomenon is also true in other contexts: for example, if two friends who are on the same wavelength, metaphorically speaking, walk down the street together, they feel stronger than if they were walking alone. Music affects us emotionally and physiologically: a sad song can make us feel sad, and an upbeat, rhythmic song can cause our heart to beat faster. Resonance can both heal and hurt.

Our mission, therefore, is to stay alert to different sounds and take the opportunity to explore tones and noises, thinking consciously about their characteristics and effects.

Jochen Fassbender, sound artist

Fire

The taming of fire was a significant development for our ancestors and led to fire being used in many different ways. Gathering around the warm hearth became a central social activity and could spark discussion and ideas. Increasingly, however, many adults have never built a fire in their lives. In order to teach children about fire, and to have respect for it, adults must first become acquainted and comfortable with it themselves.

It's not only children who enjoy working with fire

Fireplace

Grate

Natural stones

Sand

Bricks

Earth

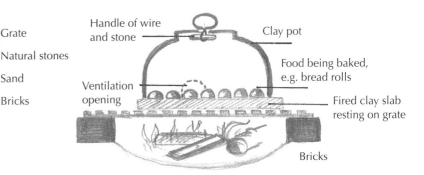

Baking oven

Handle of wire
and stone

Clay pot

Food being baked,
e.g. bread rolls

Ventilation
opening

Fired clay slab
resting on grate

Bricks

Where children are concerned, fire must be limited to small scale projects in well-planned fireplaces which can easily be kept under control. Fire is, after all, the most dangerous of the four elements. We'll look at how to create useful fires for, for example, boiling colour dyes (see the *Spring* book), cooking food (see the August chapter in this book and the *Autumn* book) or providing warmth in cold weather (see the *Winter* book).

⌐ A simple fireplace

A simple fireplace can be built with natural stones, bricks, sand and a grate (see diagram above left). This can be easily transformed into an oven for baking by adding a fired clay slab and a large clay pot as a covering hood (see diagram above right and the photograph on page 73). The basic techniques of smoking, cooking and roasting on an open fire are illustrated on page 58.

⌐ Building an underground oven

To make this underground oven, two metal buckets are welded together, and the end of one bucket is cut open to act as an oven door.

Dig a hole in the ground which will contain the fire. Place stones in it to support the oven, which sits above the fire (see below). The fire also needs

Smoking

Cooking

Roasting

58

▲ *This oven was built into a clay hill and is therefore especially well insulated*

a ventilation chimney; in the photograph above this has been built out of a tower of tin cans, tied together with wire. You could also use a clay or iron pipe.

Get the fire started, place the oven (the two buckets welded together) above it resting on the stones, and then cover the oven with earth. Bend some chicken wire so that it can slide in and out of the oven, acting as a grate for the food to be baked. Covering the grate with greased aluminium foil will protect against burning.

~ Building a clay oven

Basic fireplaces developed into clay ovens. This clay oven is made from woven willow branches (for more information on working with willow, see the *Spring* book in this series).

1. Dig out a shallow round hole, about 30–40 inches (80–100 cm) in diameter and half a spade deep.

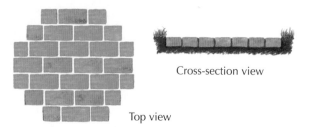

Cross-section view

Top view

2. Place bricks in the hole to make a flat base. Next, use bricks with holes in them to build an outer ring on top of the base and stick willow branches vertically into the holes.

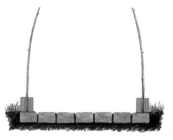

3. Tie the willow branches together at the apex with thin wire.

4. Weave the dome horizontally using thin willow branches.

5. As you weave, include a chimney in the dome, on the opposite side to the main opening.

6. Cover the willow dome with a clay and straw mixture, about 4–8 inches (10–20 cm) thick, both inside and out. The mixture should be 3 parts clay to 1 part straw. Ensure the straw is cut into very small pieces.

1

3

Don't forget:

- ✿ The main opening must at first be big enough to be able to apply the clay/straw mixture to the inside of the dome (see photograph 1).
- ✿ Afterwards, the opening can be made smaller (photograph 2). During baking, the opening is covered with a stone slab or similar.
- ✿ Quite large ovens can be built this way: photograph 4 shows one at the Children's Nature and Garden Centre.

2

4

↝ Building a clay ball oven

1. First build a solid base of broken stones or bricks, approximately 3 feet × 3 feet (1 metre × 1 metre) square and 30 inches (75 cm) high, on a frost-proof foundation.
2. Sieve about 3 cubic feet (1 cubic metre) of clay through a compost grate to get rid of large impurities.
3. Mix 5 buckets of clay, 1 bucket of finely cut straw and 1 bucket of sand in a large tub. Stir well, and add enough water so that the mixture can be shaped.
4. Make about 300 clay balls, the right size to be held in two hands.
5. Shape a pile of damp sand on the stone base to create an outline of what will be the baking area. Insert a hollow pipe to serve as a chimney at the back, and make an oven door from wood, metal or stone at the front.
6. Gently pack the clay balls around the sand dome, chimney and oven door. Blend the balls together carefully with your fingers until the oven wall is about 10 inches (25 cm) thick.

7. The oven will take 2–6 weeks to dry out, depending on the weather. You'll need to continually repair any dry cracks which appear.
8. Once the oven is completely dry, carefully remove the sand to reveal the baking space.
9. An additional roof will help protect the oven from the elements.

– A wood-fired kiln

Wouldn't it be marvellous if every kindergarten could have such a stately oven and kiln as shown here? The fire burns in the bottom section, clay is fired in the middle section and bread is baked in the top section.

The inside wall of the oven is made of fired clay bricks, and the outer wall of hard burnt bricks.

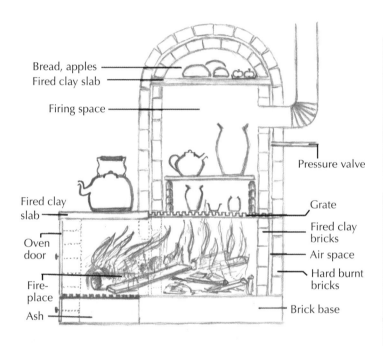

Bread, apples
Fired clay slab
Firing space
Pressure valve
Fired clay slab
Grate
Fired clay bricks
Oven door
Air space
Hard burnt bricks
Fire-place
Brick base
Ash

Between them is an insulating air space about 1 inch (2.5 cm) wide. The walls were built using special mortar. A valve connects the air space to the outside atmosphere, to help regulate the pressure.

The upper baking section can only be used when the firing temperature of around 2000°F (1100°C) has cooled to below 500°F (250°C).

Some Thoughts on Responsibility, Safety and Supervision

We're often asked, aren't the dangers of these kind of activities too great? It is indeed the case that kindergartens and schools who work closely with nature must take safety and supervision seriously. This is also true for all schools, of course, who must take responsibility for the children in their care.

Is it really that different if a child climbs a tree rather than an artificial climbing frame? Years of experience has shown that, if a child's bodily control is good enough to be able to climb a smooth trunk without help, it will be good enough for them to climb up higher and come down safely.

Of course children get wet when they play with water. You always need to have a change of clothes ready in the kindergarten, which, yes, means more work. But isn't it worth it if children feel refreshed and well-balanced after playing? The more content and peaceful they are, the less work in the long run. As for safety, as we said in the Water section children should not have access to ponds deeper than 12 inches (30 cm), and must be constantly supervised when playing near water.

Of course someone could get burned when working with fire. All fire projects must be carefully supervised by responsible adults. But it's not always the best thing to keep all dangers away from children. Sometimes, the best way to learn is to touch something hot, and know not to do it again because it hurts. If children (or indeed adults) are scared of fire, they're more likely to panic and hurt themselves; helping them gain confidence with fire in a safe environment will protect them more.

We thoroughly recommend that any adults who work with children should take an appropriate first aid course, and subsequent refresher courses to keep their skills up to date. Adults will be more confident if they know how to handle a potentially dangerous situation.

Parents should also be encouraged to let their children play in natural surroundings. Playing

near a brook, lighting a fire to cook a simple meal or playing in mud are all activities that children won't forget. The feeling of sleeping in a tent on a warm summer night and waking the next morning to singing birds, humming insects and dew on the grass: these experiences will stay with them much longer than the most luxurious hotel stay in an exotic location. Our immediate environments offer so many beautiful spots, just waiting to be discovered. They're closer than you think!

Barley at harvest time

Mother Earth
Eileen Hutchins

Mother Earth,
Mother Earth,
Take our seed
And give it birth.

Father Sun,
Gleam and glow,
Until the roots
Begin to grow.

Sister Rain,
Sister Rain,
Shed thy tears
To swell the grain.

Brother Wind,
Breathe and blow
Then the blade
Green will grow.

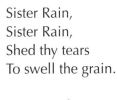

Earth and Sun,
And wind and rain,
Turn to gold
The living grain.

August

From Grain to Bread

The grain kernels are loosened from the ears with a round piece of wood

These children are learning to thresh the harvest with a flail, an ancient hand tool used for threshing

The growth of seeds and fruit mark the period under the zodiac sign of Leo the lion (Ω). This is a time when the sun powerfully illuminates the earth, just as the royal lion rules over his kingdom.

In the fields, the grain ears become ready for harvesting. They start to lean over as the grain kernels grow ripe with living seeds. Our work back in March (see the *Spring* book) in planting the seeds has now to come fruition: nature has rewarded our efforts. To many people's amazement, the grain stalks will have grown very high: up to 6 feet (2 metres) in some cases. They'd grow this high in conventional fields as well if they weren't treated with growth retardants.

The grain should be carefully cut just above the ground and tied into sheaves. Put the bundles on display in the kindergarten for a while, so the children can examine their harvest. In the following days, cut the ears off the stalks, lay them individually on a wooden slab and thresh them with a piece of round wood until the grain kernels come out (as show in the photograph at the top of this page).

Collect the kernels in a container. Each one is precious; not a single one should go to waste. Divide up the harvest into three parts: save one third as seeds to plant the following spring; grind one third into flour with a manual grain mill or coffee mill, for use in the thanksgiving bread later; and get some strong children to pound the final third into grain flakes, using wooden slabs and round pieces of wood.

Grinding grain into flour is particularly good activity for restless or hyperactive children, and can help develop patience. Even kindergartens with only a small space can manage it with some careful planning. Above all, working with grain helps children to make the connection between planting a seed, harvesting the crop and turning it

into daily bread or cereal. It's important that children know where their food comes from — and are able to make the link between what they've done themselves, and the work of a combine harvester which reaps miles and miles of grain.

All aspects of a child — physical, mental and emotional — are fully engaged when using a manual grain mill

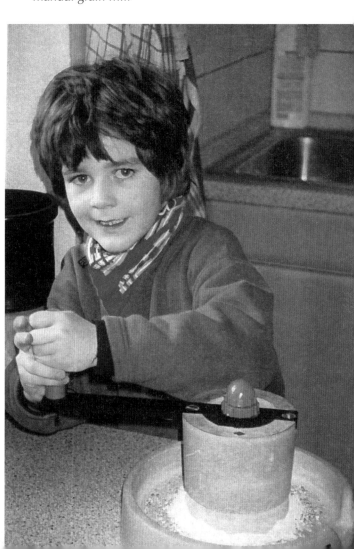

Healthy Nourishment

Our prosperous society often undervalues the importance of nourishment. Food and drink are seen as sources of enjoyment rather than something that keeps us healthy. With grain, for example, the most valuable part — the kernel — is normally removed, so that the flour will last longer (the high fat content of the kernel means it can go bad quite quickly). Superfine flour, or most types of regular white flour, has had the kernel — the bran and the wheat germ — removed. All that is left is the white starchy part of the grain; the vitamin- and fibre-rich parts have been lost. This is one reason for the increase in illnesses caused by poor nutrition.

Our food supplies are also out of balance. Many people in the third world starve while those in the first world are growing more obese. The huge consumption of meat in the first world is

Give Us This Day Our Daily Bread

At some point in our history, human beings settled into farming. They domesticated animals and bred crops from wild plants. They took what nature gave them and cultivated it. Until the advent of industrialization in the nineteenth century, this way of life stayed largely the same and was the centre of human society. There was a mutual give and take between human beings and nature.

Today's modern farming methods try to force agriculture into economically-predictable systems. In doing so, we forget about the living plants, the living animals, and the human input. Biodynamic agriculture, in contrast, tries to restore some of the balance. It prioritizes care of the earth, respect for nature and the food it gives us, and a proper integration of these values into human culture.

Christians regularly pray, "give us this day our daily bread." We must remember that bread is indeed a gift, and we should accept it gratefully.

Stefan Roth, biodynamic farmer

At the Centre we use a mill that the children can work manually, but which also runs off electricity for adult use

partly to blame for both situations: a large part of the world's grain harvest is fed to cattle, where only one-seventh of its nourishment is converted into meat. The food of the poor serves as feed for the cattle of the rich.

Industrialized farming also causes serious ecological damage. Huge areas are used to grow just a single plant which has been especially bred to be high-yield. This approach requires a large amount of fertilizer and pesticide, and the doses must be constantly increased: pests become resistant, ground erosion increases, and groundwater supplies are threatened by pollutants. Somehow, this vicious circle must be broken.

Fortunately, there is an increasing awareness of the dangers, and more and more farms are switching to organic and biodynamic food production, largely because of consumer demand. Our children must also understand the issues involved, so that in turn they can continue to improve the situation; this is best done through a positive reinforcement of the joys of growing, caring for and harvesting plants and making food, rather than scaring them with possible horror stories.

All cultures and religions have, until now, believed that a higher power is responsible for preserving the natural basis of life. The following graces and table blessings reflect this:

All good gifts around us
Are sent from heaven above
So thank the Lord, so thank the Lord
For all his love. Amen.

Thank you for the world so sweet, bom bom,
Thank you for the food we eat, yum yum,
Thank you for the birds that sing-a-ling-a-ling
Thank you God for everything.

Grinding kernels using stones

Simple food like fresh peppermint tea, herb butter, herb cheese, herb salt and bread becomes a banquet when all the food is homemade

A core aim of any kindergarten should be to make children — and their parents — aware of what food they eat, and how food can keep them healthy. Years of experience has shown that wholesome food, freshly prepared in the kindergarten every day with the help of the children, is one of the best ways to teach children to enjoy a wide range of food, and to appreciate the value of good nourishment.

▼ *A portable baking oven at a medieval fair*

A weekly baking day at a kindergarten. An understanding of nourishment at this age is best achieved through a love of food, experienced with all the senses.

Creating an Eating Culture

Preparing a fresh meal involves all the senses, from handling and smelling the food to seeing how good it looks when ready to eat. Cooking is an especially good way of developing children's motor skills, through mixing, kneading, shaping, cutting and setting the table. Learning about cooking in an abstract, educationally-sanitized way is no substitute for doing the real thing.

Many children these days receive all their meals, apart from evening supper, at school, and so schools and kindergartens have an obligation to provide the best quality nourishment possible. Pre-prepared processed food warmed up in a microwave is simply not good enough. The examples that follow show that it is perfectly possible to provide a healthy snack and fresh lunch on a daily basis without too much expense. Indeed, the real cost comes later if children get ill or can't concentrate because of a poor diet.

Dough is made from flour, water, a pinch of salt and lots of fresh garden herbs …

… rolls are shaped …

A daily snack time nearly always proves very popular with children. Allowing for allergies or special dietary needs, the snack could just be fruit, vegetables or salad, sometimes supplemented with tea, milk or fruit juice. When a whole class eats together, eating becomes part of the culture of that group. A grace or blessing can be used where appropriate, with everyone holding hands; this helps to make the snack time something special, apart from the daily routine, and helps to develop rich language skills.

There's hardly an activity that doesn't go better when accompanied by music. This song provides a good rhythm for grinding, kneading and shaping:

… and placed under the clay dome of a baking oven

The Swing

1 How do you like to go up in a swing, up in the air so blue?___
2 Up to the air___ and o - ver the wall, till I can see so wide, ___
3 Till I look down on the gar - den green, down on the roof so brown,___

O, I do think it the pleas - ant - est thing ev - er a child can do!___
riv - ers and trees___ and cat - tle and all o - ver the coun - try - side___
up in the air I go fly - ing a - gain, up in the air and down!___

From Whole Grain to Fine Flour: the Story of Grain

Wheat, rye, barley, oats, spelt, corn, millet and rice all belong to the grass family, and have been cultivated as crops since the stone age. Our ancestors harvested the kernels and ate them raw, which was good for the teeth. As their culture developed, they learned to dry the harvest and store provisions for the winter. They put the kernels into a piece of hollowed-out stone and rubbed them with a smaller stone to create a kind of wholemeal flour.

When the Romans went on a crusade, they took grain and grain mills along with them, so that they could eat independently of their surroundings for weeks or months. They baked bread with the ground flour, using left-over sourdough from the last baking as leavening. The sourdough was added to the flour together with water and salt, and kneaded into a smooth mass. Today, we can buy sourdough from many bakeries and health food stores.

— Sourdough bread

Mix 18 oz (500 g) of rye flour with 1 pint (500 ml) of water and 2–4 tablespoons of sourdough. Cover and leave to stand for 8 hours, then add 1 lb (500 g) of wheat flour, 1 teaspoon of salt and about 1/2 pint (250 ml) of water. Add the water gradually and stop when the dough is of kneading consistency. Knead the dough well and place it in a loaf tin. Leave to rise in a warm place for about 90 minutes.

In earlier days, while the bread was rising the baking oven would be fired up with twigs and

A large professional baking oven

pieces of wood. The temperature was checked using a piece of straw: if the straw turned to ashes immediately, the oven was hot enough.

The coals were drawn out of the oven on a flat board, and the oven cleaned with wet straw. The loaf of bread was then pushed in on a wooden board. After 90 minutes, if the bread had a nice brown crust, it was "refreshed", that is, taken out of the tin and brushed with cold water, before being put back into the oven for another 10 minutes to develop a crisp crust all over and a nice sheen. Loaves could be stored in a cool cellar, on a board hanging below the ceiling, for up to three weeks.

The development of water mills and windmills meant that a finer flour could be produced, and so the variety of grain products available increased hugely, using ingredients like bran, hulled barley grain, oatmeal flakes and fine starch meal. Today, alongside a hundred or more different types of bread, we can make cakes, cookies, waffles, dumplings, pasta and noodles, corn flakes, puddings and lots, lots more.

Ruth Hecht

Grain Recipes

— Whole grains: wheat, rye, barley or oats

Amount per person: $1/3$ to $1/2$ cup (1 handful or 100 ml)

Wash the grain well and leave to stand in water for 10–12 hours. Boil one part grain with three parts water without salt for about 15 minutes, then pour into a thermos flask or large pot and leave to expand for 3–4 hours. (If salt is used, the grain won't become soft.) If the grain isn't left to stand overnight, increase the boiling time by $1 1/2$ to 2 hours. Before serving, heat briefly and season to taste. The grain can be left on a low heat for up to an hour before serving.

Salty grain tastes especially good with vegetables or salad, and can also be baked with cheese and freshly chopped herbs. Alternatively, grain can be sweetened with milk and honey after heating, or eaten with dried fruit or apple sauce. It's especially good as a kindergarten snack: wholegrain food which hasn't been chopped or ground encourages strong chewing and healthy saliva, which in turn supports healthy teeth.

— Millet porridge (serves 4)

$1 1/2$ cups (375 ml) of millet
3 cups (750 ml) of water
$1 1/2$ cups (375 ml) of milk
1 teaspoon of honey or syrup
raisins (optional)

Boil the millet briefly in some water, then pour into a sieve and rinse well, to remove the bitter taste. Put back in the pan and simmer gently with the amount of water given above, until the water is absorbed (about 10–15 minutes). Add the milk, and raisins if desired, heat quickly, then cover and allow to expand. Add sweetening to taste.

— Bread and rolls

This recipe makes two loaves and 30 rolls, enough for a kindergarten class.

Mix together $4 1/2$ lb (2 kg) of wheat flour, $2 1/4$ lb (1 kg) of rye flour and 3 tablespoons of salt. Leave the bowl in a warm place. Heat 4 pints (2 l) of buttermilk, kefir or sour milk to 99°F (37°C). Mix 1 cup (300 ml) of the liquid with 6 oz (180 g) of yeast, then mix the liquid and the yeast mixture into the dry ingredients to form a dough. Cover and leave to stand in a warm place for about 15 minutes. Knead the dough, leave to stand for another 30 minutes, then knead again. Divide the dough into three parts to make two loaves in loaf tins, and 30 bread rolls.

Bake the rolls at 400°F (200°C) for 30–40 minutes, or until golden brown. During this time, the loaves will rise; then bake them at 400°F (200°C) for 60–70 minutes. During baking, place a shallow bowl with water into the oven, to stop the rolls and loaves from becoming too hard.

Variation: for sweet rolls, add raisins or other dried fruit marinated in buttermilk, and knead into the dough.

— Flat bread

Flat bread doesn't contain any yeast to make it rise and so is easy to make.

Grind wheat kernels into flour using a coffee mill or grain mill. Add a pinch of salt and enough water to form a dough. Form flat loaves the size of your hand and bake them on a hot stone in a fireplace.

Baking stick bread. An inner ring made of branches supported on wood helps children to keep their sticks of bread in place above the fire.

The dough will keep its shape during baking if it has been wound round the stick in a careful spiral

⌐ Basic dough for fruit cake, pretzels, cookies and pizza

This dough is best made from freshly-ground wholegrain flour.
1 lb (500 g) of flour
4 oz (120 g) of white cheese or ricotta
2 1/2 oz (70 g) of margarine, butter or oil
1 cup (300 ml) of warm water
1/2 teaspoon of salt
For sweet dough, add 1–2 tablespoons of honey or pear syrup
For savoury or pizza dough, add freshly chopped herbs

Mix the ingredients together to form a dough. It's well-suited to use in kindergartens because it doesn't stick to the hands or the table.

⌐ Stick bread

1 lb (500 g) of whole grain flour
3/4 oz (20 g) of yeast
1 pint (500 ml) of water
2 teaspoons of salt
2 1/4 oz (60 g) of butter

Knead the yeast dough, roll it out and cut into long strips. Wrap the dough strips around a long stick and bake over the coals of an open fire.

A Quick Reminder

In August, flowers, grasses and branches should be collected for advent wreaths and bouquets, and hung up to dry (see *Winter* book in this series).

This is also the time to collect and dry the seeds from ox-tongues, grasses, nettles and other wild and garden plants; they can be used as bird feed later in the year (also see the *Winter* book).

The Pancake Mill

Once upon a time there was an old man and an old woman who were farmers. They were very poor and had a hard life. One day, they didn't have a crumb of bread left in the house, so they went into the woods to gather acorns. They brought the acorns home and started to eat them.

As they were eating, the old woman dropped one onto the ground. It fell through a crack in the floor, into the cellar. Soon, the acorn grew roots and a shoot, and in no time the shoot had grown up to the floor above. The old woman saw this and said to the old man, "Look, you need to make a hole in the floor so that the oak tree can grow. When it gets big enough, we'll be able to pick the acorns right here in the room, and we won't have to go into the woods."

So the old man made a hole in the floor, and the oak tree grew and grew. It grew right up to the ceiling of the room, from the ceiling to the roof, and from the roof to the sky.

When they had next run out of acorns, the old man took a sack and climbed up the oak tree. He climbed higher and higher to reach the top, collecting acorns along the way. Suddenly, he found himself in heaven. He walked around and saw a rooster with a golden comb, sitting on top of a golden grain mill.

The farmer didn't think for very long. He took the rooster and the golden mill, and climbed back down. When he arrived home, he asked the old woman, "What's for supper?"

"Wait, I'll grind the acorns in the mill," said the old woman. As the rooster watched, she took the golden mill and began to grind. And guess what came out? Pancakes and pastries! As often as she turned the mill handle, a pancake and a pastry came out.

Now, the old couple had enough to eat.

One day, a gentleman came by and said, "I'm very hungry. Do you have anything to eat?"

"Of course," they said, "you can have some of our pancakes." The rooster and the gentleman watched as the old woman turned the handle on the golden mill and out came pancakes and pastries. The gentleman enjoyed eating them very much. After the meal, he said, "Woman, sell me the mill!"

"No, I can't sell it," she replied.

But the gentleman wanted the mill, so he stole it and left. When the old couple saw that the mill had gone, they were very unhappy. "Don't be unhappy," said the rooster with the golden comb. "I'll fly after the thief and catch him."

The rooster flew to the big house, perched on the gate and called out, "Cock-a-doodle-do! I'm here now! Sir, please give us back our precious golden mill!"

When the gentleman heard the rooster, he was very angry and ordered, "Throw the rooster into the water!" His servants grabbed the rooster and threw it into the well. But the rooster said to himself, "Little beak, little beak, drink the water!" He drank and drank until the well was empty and flew back to the big house. He perched on the balcony and called out, "Cock-a-doodle-do! I'm here again! Sir, please give us back our precious golden mill!"

The gentleman ordered the rooster to be caught and thrown into a hot oven. His servants grabbed the rooster and threw it into the fire. But the rooster said to himself, "Little beak, little beak, spit out the water!" He spit all the water out into the oven, and put out the fire.

Then he stretched himself, shook himself, and flew out of the oven, screaming, "Cock-a-doodle-do! I'm here once again! Sir, please give us back our precious golden mill!"

Finally the guests at the big house heard this and were scared. They ran out of the house, and the gentleman ran after them. The rooster with the golden comb saw his chance, flew in and picked up the golden mill. He flew back to the old couple's house with it, and they were very glad to see him. From now on, they promised, they would take good care of the golden mill. And they enjoyed pancakes and pastries for the rest of their lives.

77

Resources

Further reading

General

Brigitte Barz, *Festivals with Children,* Floris, Edinburgh

Joseph Cornell, *Sharing Nature with Children,* Dawn, California

Freya Jaffke, *Work and Play in Early Childhood,* Floris, Edinburgh

Sally Jenkinson, *The Genius of Play,* Hawthorn, Stroud

Martin Large, *Set Free Childhood,* Hawthorn, Stroud

Nancy Mellon, *Storytelling with Children,* Hawthorn, Stroud

Rudolf Meyer, *The Wisdom of Fairy Tales,* Floris, Edinburgh

Lynne Oldfield, *Free to Learn,* Hawthorn, Stroud

Activities with the elements

Petra Berger, *Crafts Through the Year,* Floris, Edinburgh

Walter Kraul, *Earth, Water, Fire and Air: Playful Explorations in the Four Elements,* Floris, Edinburgh

M. van Leeuwen, *The Nature Corner,* Floris, Edinburgh

Carol Petrash, *Earthwise: Environmental Crafts and Activities With Young Children,* Floris, Edinburgh (in North America: *Earthways: Simple Environmental Activities for Young Children,* Gryphon, Beltsville MD)

Anne and Peter Thomas, *The Big Summer Activity Book,* Floris, Edinburgh

CHLADNI PLATES AND CYMATICS FOR ADULTS

Hans Jenny, *Cymatics: A Study of Wave Phenomena and Vibration,* Macromedia, Newmarket NH

Alexander Lauterwasser: *Water Sound Images: The Creative Music of the Universe,* Macromedia, Newmarket NH

Butterflies for children (non-fiction)

Butterflies, Usborne Spotters Guide, London

Stephanie Turnbull, *Caterpillars and Butterflies,* Usborne Beginners Series, London

Cooking and nutrition

Wendy Cook, *The Biodynamic Food and Cookbook,* Clairview, Sussex

—, *Foodwise: Understanding what we eat and how it affects us,* Clairview, Sussex

Lisa Hildreth, *The Waldorf Kindergarten Snack Book,* Rudolf Steiner Press

Jekka McVicar, *New Book of Herbs,* Dorling Kindersley, London

For organic herb supplies in the UK, visit Jekka's Herb Farm online at *www.jekkasherbfarm.com* or The Organic Herb Trading Co. at *www.organicherbtrading.co.uk.* There is also a good list of suppliers at *www.aboutorganics.co.uk*

In North America, visit the Organic Consumers Association at *www.organicconsumers.org* or the Natural Food Network at *www.naturalfoodnet.com* for a list of organic suppliers.

Story books, poetry and songs

Elsa Beskow, *Peter in Blueberry Land,* Floris, Edinburgh

—, *Christopher's Harvest Time,* Floris, Edinburgh

Daniel C. Bryan, *The Nettle and the Butterfly,* Wynstones Press, Stourbridge

Eric Carle, *The Very Hungry Caterpillar,* Puffin, London

Warren Lee Cohen, *Dragon Baked Bread,* Temple Lodge, Sussex

Loek Koopmans, *The Pancake That Ran Away,* Floris, Edinburgh

—, *The Apple Cake,* Floris, Edinburgh

Reeve Lindbergh (ed.), *In Every Tiny Grain of Sand,* Walker, London

Brien Masters, *The Waldorf Song Book*, Floris,
Edinburgh
Gerda Muller, *Summer* (board book without text),
Floris, Edinburgh
Ann Pilling, *Before I go to sleep*, Kingfisher, London
Marlys Swinger (ed.), *Sing through the Day*, Plough,
New York & Sussex
Marlys Swinger (ed.), *Sing through the Seasons*,
Plough, New York & Sussex
Heather Thomas, *A Journey Through Time in Verse
and Rhyme*, Floris, Edinburgh

The Children's Nature and Garden Centre

The Children's Nature and Garden Centre in Reichshof
is open to all and offers seasonal nature classes. The
Centre works closely with kindergartens and schools,
and with parents. Its grounds are well equipped for
practical, hands-on workshops, seminars and extended
courses, and it also offers advice and support for those
who want to set up similar schemes elsewhere.

For more information, contact the Centre at:

Natur-Kinder-Garten-Werkstatt Reichshof
Dorner Weg 4
51580 Reichshof
Germany

Tel: +49-22 61-52 22 1
Fax: +49-22 61-80 48 31

irmgardkutsch@aol.com
http://www.natur-kinder-garten-werkstatt.de

Credits
Photographs and illustrations

Edgar Bayer: p. 60; Tijmen van Dobbenburgh: p. 30
(II); Max Eisl: p. 27(II); Jochen Fassbender: p. 55 (I)
Jens Frank: p. 25 (II); Martina Frechen: p. 48 (I);
Marianne Frielingsdorf: p. 22 (I), 25 (I); Jan Gese: p.
11 (I); Brad Harrison: p. 65; Horst Heindrichs: p. 22
(II); Fritz Hilgenstock: p. 51 (I, III); Ulf Hinze: p. 6,
18; Paul Joseph: p. 37 (II); Kindergarten Kotthausen:
p. 9 (I); Ingeborg Ludwig-Kersjes: p. 26, 50 (I); Peter
Lange: p. 36 (II); Ute Lübert: p. 7, 69 (I, III); Gerd
Marstedt: p. 43 (II); Ute Poeppel: p. 43 (I); Marcel
Reimer: p. 17; Erika Salaw: p. 34 (III), 69 (II), 72
(I); H.-G. Schrohe, Foto-Atelier Bestgen: p. 33 (III);
Gerhard Sturm: p. 32 (I–IV), 33 (II), 37 (I); Christian
Tangemann: p. 21 (IV), 44 (I), 62 (I–IV), 70, 71 (I), 72
(II, III), 73; Mark Tasco: p. 30 (I), 31 (II); Ove Tøpfer:
p. 42 (II); Brigitte Walden: p. 52 (I), 55 (II, III), 58;
Waldorfkindergarten Zaunkönig, Remscheid: 41 (I,
II); Wikipedia: p. 22 (III), 27 (I); Anke Wilhelm: p. 16,
17, 21 (III, IV), 23, 40, 56, 57 (I,II), 63, 68 (I); Carolin
Winkendick: p. 21 (I, II)

All other photographs by Irmgard Kutsch

Special thanks

Thanks to the Nature and Environmental Protection
Academy of North-Rhine Westphalia for the Herb
Alphabet on pages 18–19. And thanks to Marianne
Frielingsdorf for the delicious herb recipes on
pages 22–27

Nature Activities for All Seasons

SPRING
nature activities for children

Irmgard Kutsch & Brigitte Walden

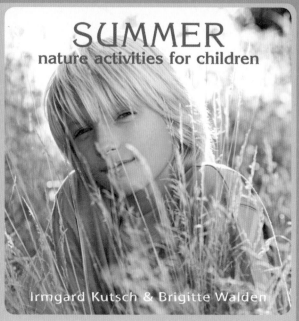

SUMMER
nature activities for children

Irmgard Kutsch & Brigitte Walden

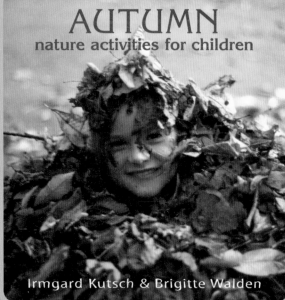

AUTUMN
nature activities for children

Irmgard Kutsch & Brigitte Walden

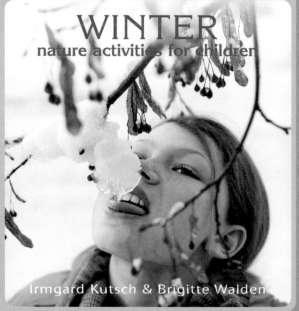

WINTER
nature activities for children

Irmgard Kutsch & Brigitte Walden